U.S.-CHINA CYBERSECURITY ISSUES

ROUNDTABLE

BEFORE THE

U.S.-CHINA ECONOMIC AND SECURITY REVIEW COMMISSION

ONE HUNDRED THIRTEENTH CONGRESS
FIRST SESSION

THURSDAY, JULY 11, 2013

Printed for use of the
United States-China Economic and Security Review Commission
Available via the World Wide Web: www.uscc.gov

UNITED STATES-CHINA ECONOMIC AND SECURITY REVIEW COMMISSION

WASHINGTON: 2013

U.S.-CHINA ECONOMIC AND SECURITY REVIEW COMMISSION

Hon. WILLIAM A. REINSCH, *Chairman*
Hon. DENNIS C. SHEA, Vice *Chairman*

Commissioners:

CAROLYN BARTHOLOMEW	DANIEL M. SLANE
PETER BROOKES	SEN. JAMES TALENT
ROBIN CLEVELAND	DR. KATHERINE C. TOBIN
JEFFREY L. FIEDLER	MICHAEL R. WESSEL
SEN. CARTE P. GOODWIN	DR. LARRY M. WORTZEL

MICHAEL R. DANIS, *Executive Director*

The Commission was created on October 30, 2000 by the Floyd D. Spence National Defense Authorization Act for 2001 § 1238, Public Law No. 106-398, 114 STAT. 1654A-334 (2000) (codified at 22 U.S.C. § 7002 (2001), as amended by the Treasury and General Government Appropriations Act for 2002 § 645 (regarding employment status of staff) & § 648 (regarding changing annual report due date from March to June), Public Law No. 107-67, 115 STAT. 514 (Nov. 12, 2001); as amended by Division P of the "Consolidated Appropriations Resolution, 2003," Pub L. No. 108-7 (Feb. 20, 2003) (regarding Commission name change, terms of Commissioners, and responsibilities of the Commission); as amended by Public Law No. 109-108 (H.R. 2862) (Nov. 22, 2005) (regarding responsibilities of Commission and applicability of FACA); as amended by Division J of the "Consolidated Appropriations Act, 2008," Public Law Nol. 110-161 (December 26, 2007) (regarding responsibilities of the Commission, and changing the Annual Report due date from June to December).

The Commission's full charter is available at www.uscc.gov.

July 22, 2013

The Honorable Patrick J. Leahy
President Pro Tempore of the Senate, Washington, D.C. 20510
The Honorable John A. Boehner
Speaker of the House of Representatives, Washington, D.C. 20515

DEAR SENATOR LEAHY AND SPEAKER BOEHNER:

We are pleased to notify you of the Commission's July 11, 2013 public roundtable on *"U.S.-China Cybersecurity Issues."* The Floyd D. Spence National Defense Authorization Act (amended by Pub. L. No. 109-108, section 635(a)) provides the basis for this roundtable.

At the roundtable, the Commissioners' discussed relevant and critical cybersecurity topics with the following participants: Mr. Roy Kamphausen, Senior Advisor for Political and Security Affairs at the National Bureau of Asian Research and Deputy Executive Director for the Commission on the Theft of American Intellectual Property; Dr. James Mulvenon, Vice President, Intelligence Division, Defense Group Inc.; and Mr. Bruce Quinn, Rockwell Automation's Vice President for Government Relations and former Chief Representative of Rockwell Automation in China. The roundtable identified and explored potential U.S. actions and policies that could prompt Beijing to change its approach to cyberspace and deter future Chinese cyber theft.

We note that the roundtable transcript will soon be available on the Commission's website at www.USCC.gov. Members and the staff of the Commission are available to provide more detailed briefings. We hope these materials will be helpful to the Congress as it continues its assessment of U.S.-China relations and their impact on U.S. security.

The Commission will examine in greater depth these issues, and the other issues enumerated in its statutory mandate, in its 2013 Annual Report that will be submitted to Congress in November 2013. Should you have any questions regarding this roundtable or any other issue related to China, please do not hesitate to have your staff contact our Congressional Liaison, Reed Eckhold, at (202) 624-1496 or via email at reckhold@uscc.gov.

Sincerely yours,

Hon. William A. Reinsch
Chairman

Hon. Dennis C. Shea
Vice Chairman

U.S.-CHINA CYBERSECURITY ISSUES

THURSDAY, JULY 11, 2013

———————

U.S.-CHINA ECONOMIC AND SECURITY REVIEW COMMISSION

Washington, D.C.

The Commission met in Russell Senate Office Building, Room SR-328A, Washington, D.C. at 9:00 a.m., Commissioners William Reinsch, Dennis Shea, and Michael Wessel, presiding. Roundtable participants were Bruce Quinn, Rockwell Automation's Vice President for Government Relations and former Chief Representative of Rockwell Automation in China; Mr. Roy Kamphausen, Senior Advisor for Political and Security Affairs at the National Bureau of Asian Research and Deputy Executive Director for the Commission on the Theft of American Intellectual Property; and Dr. James Mulvenon, Vice President, Intelligence Division, Defense Group Inc.

———————————————————————————

CHAIRMAN REINSCH: Welcome everybody, we're going to begin. You can tell from the arrangement that this is informal, at least as informal as we ever get. This is a roundtable on U.S.-China cyber security issues. A roundtable means we don't have witnesses, *per se*, and prepared testimony or time limits. I don't even have a gavel so we're not going to gavel you down after seven minutes.

And we've got our Commissioners, more of whom I hope will be arriving, interspersed with our guests who are experts on the subject. I want to say a word about the format, and then I'll introduce our guests.

As I said, it's a roundtable so we're not asking for prepared statements or testimony. We're going to have a discussion, and the topic is one step beyond what's going on in the cyber intrusion world because there have been zillions of hearings about that and thousands of pages of testimony. We want to focus today on what do we do about it, particularly with respect to China. A few guiding questions are as follows:

- What can we do about it diplomatically?
- What can we do about it legally?
- What can we do about it economically?
- What can we do about it from any perspective that you want to address, and what are the implications of the various proposals or suggestions that you might make for action or diplomatic activity or whatever?

So this allows us to skip the long opening statements about the things the Chinese are doing and instead go directly to how do we deal with it, and hopefully we'll have a good discussion on that.

We have with us three significant experts and very knowledgeable people on the subject. I should say in the beginning that we had a fourth who was listed, Catherine Lotrionte, who unfortunately had a family medical emergency and couldn't be with us this morning, something that came up last night. But we are privileged to have with us three other people who I know will more than fill the gap that she leaves, and I want to say a few words about each of them.

First, we have--and this in alphabetical order, not order of importance or anything else-- Roy Kamphausen, who is a Senior Advisor for Political and Security Affairs at the National Bureau of Asian Research and was the Deputy Executive Director of the Commission on the Theft of American Intellectual Property, which issued a report fairly recently.

Prior to joining NBR, he served as a U.S. Army officer, a career that culminated in an assignment in the Office of the Secretary of Defense as the Country Director for China-Taiwan-Mongolia Affairs.

We also have with us James Mulvenon, who is Vice President of Defense Group Incorporated's Intelligence Division and Director of DGI's Center for Intelligence Research and Analysis. He is also a founding member and current President of the Cyber Conflict Studies Association. He received his Ph.D. in political science from the University of California, Los Angeles.

Dr. Mulvenon has also been a frequent witness so we're glad to have you here as well in a less formal capacity.

And third, we have Bruce Quinn, who is Vice President for Government Relations at Rockwell Automation, and previously served as Rockwell's Chief Representative in China. Rockwell is a company with substantial experience in this area.

So we're very happy to have all of you here. I also want to particularly thank Chairman Stabenow and the staff of the Senate Agriculture Committee for providing today's venue. We're very grateful for that and for arranging things in a way that we could have an informal conversation.

So let me also say to our guests out there in the audience that we put index cards by the stack of reports at the table in the rear. If you have a question that you want me to ask, feel free to write it on the index card and leave it there. Periodically one of our staff will bring them up. No guarantees that you'll make the cut and it will be asked, but if you want to have a question, something that pops into your mind, write it down, leave it there, and if we have time, as things roll on, we'll get to them.

We, however, have prepared some questions, some of which we've slipped to our guests in advance, so it won't be a complete surprise. The way that I'd like to proceed is I'm going to ask a question, and then at least for the first one ask our three guests to make a few comments about it, and then we'll have a discussion. Commissioners can weigh in as you see fit.

When we run out of gas, I'll ask another question or you can ask another question or, guests, you can ask questions of each other. If you want to say to one of them, boy, that's a really stupid idea, feel free, and we'll have a discussion from that.

I don't think we'll run out of questions because this is a hot topic that a number of Commissioners have given a lot of thought to and which the Commission itself has spent a good bit of time on over the years. So there is ample material.

So with that, let me go to the first question unless there are any amendments from other commissioners? Okay. The first question, which, as I've said, we've slipped to them in advance, is basically a reformulation of what I just said: what actions and policies should the U.S. government implement to curtail future Chinese cyber theft? And related, how will these actions and policies affect the broader U.S.-China relationship, which, of course, is one of the things we have to think about before we take any steps?

So why don't we just open that up and let's begin with Roy, and we'll just go in the order in which I introduced you if that's all right, and then after that, it's a free for all.

And, please, yes, push your talk button when you want to talk and push it off when you stop.

MR. KAMPHAUSEN: Well, Mr. Chairman, it's a pleasure to be here today and to be a part of this discussion. I should say that I will hopefully represent the Commission's views well, and--

CHAIRMAN REINSCH: Your Commission; not our Commission.

MR. KAMPHAUSEN: The IP Commission's views; right--so that we talk about what they thought were the most important conclusions from that year-long effort and probably keep my own views to a minimum.

So I think the Commission would say in regard to the first question maybe three things. First, to understand the nature of the problem, and they were at great pains throughout the process that we undertook for a year to understand that cyber was part of a bigger whole in the theft of American intellectual property. It's a means to an end. We talk often in the report about cyber-enabled theft, and, interestingly, the administration has begun to use similar sort of terminology.

The first point is cyber is part of a bigger whole, and if we overfixate or overfocus on the problem, we may miss some other things.

The second, their major driving impetus for how they thought about the problem and how to solve it and really the work of the Commission was less about admiring the problem and more about what we do about it and so right in keeping with the thrust of the meeting today.

They said we've really got to leverage American strengths and those things which are desired by international companies that aspire to be global companies. Then we've got to make clear that to operate in the American market, to use the American banking system and so forth, you have to play by the rules as they are laid out. So much less apologetic for our system and more recognizing that we have strengths in our system that others want to leverage and take advantage of. In order to do that, they need to play by the rules.

The third, and this, I think, pertains more directly to the question of cyber, but really applies to all aspects of the theft of intellectual property more broadly, the third point is to say we've got to change the cost-benefit calculus of those that are seeking to steal what it is that American companies have or, in other cases, the U.S. government and national security secrets and so forth.

And this really, I think, opens the door to the recommendations that the Commission had, and maybe I'll take a break and then return to those, but specifically on cyber, what they said was the environment is changing. To make the theft, using cyber means, of intellectual property more costly requires us to think more broadly about how we can conceive of and develop the rules that govern behavior in the cyber domain.

Some have taken that to mean--in fact, the New York Times piece the day that we launched the report said Commission recommends offensive cyber. Yet in fact, the commissioners said quite clearly we don't recommend that, but we understand that given the nature of the environment and how it's changing, we may find ourselves in a world in which companies and others begin to take matters into their own hands because they sense that there is nothing that's being done on their behalf.

So I can talk about that maybe in more detail in a minute, but I'll give others a chance to talk as well.

CHAIRMAN REINSCH: Good. James.

DR. MULVENON: Well, first of all, when a policymaker five years ago had asked me that question, my answer was, ma'am, we have an attribution problem. We don't know whether that is definitively a Chinese military intrusion actor or a Romanian hacking through a Chinese server and coming to the United States.

We worked that problem very hard for three years, and we no longer have an attribution problem. We have scads of attribution. In many ways, we have too much attribution. Now that's not to say that there won't be false flag and other sort of evolutions of that issue, but that is not the problem anymore. We spent the last two years thinking about what to do about it.

And a variety of things were offered along the way, basically in four main buckets. One was somebody said, well, why don't we simply, you know, it's like nuclear weapons, let's just have a deterrence policy, you know, and then people will be deterred. But saying it doesn't make it so. It's a lot harder than that. We have to have some Cuban missile crises and Berlin airlifts along the way to establish the credibility of that deterrent, and as long as some of our more sensitive capabilities remain obscured, it's very difficult to establish that kind of a deterrent.

Other people say, oh, this is just a defense problem. It's just a question of buying a different firewall and adding more anti-virus products and things along those lines. And as someone who has looked at this issue for a long time at the operational level, I can tell you the offense will always have the advantage. If they only have to find one way to get in, the defense has to find every way to stop them.

And, in fact, the more sophisticated people who look at this issue have now adopted a completely new mind-set which says perimeter defense is impossible. You're going to have advanced persistent threat in your network at all times, you're going to have compromised hardware and software in your system at all times, or you should assume that you do. Therefore, you need to come up with strategies, and there's been some very clever things that people have come up with for how you operate inside a compromised system. So defense is not the answer.

Other people say let's just scare them straight, you know, let's just go steal their stuff, and then we'll come to some sort of an equilibrium, some sort of Moscow rules. And as the father of two teenage daughters, I sympathize with this "scare them straight" philosophy, you know, take them to a juvenile detention center, let them meet some of the residents, you know, maybe they'll start obeying their mother.

But the problem is that the Chinese already believe that we're ubiquitously intruding their networks. So you're not changing a mind-set, and that's absolutely critical.

So the final thing that we've been looking at, and the one that really has had the greatest traction, I think, in terms of Roy's point about changing the cost-benefit calculus--which, by the way, the Chinese have to come to that conclusion themselves--we're not going to be able to hector them through a demarche or some sort of a criticism or a Mandiant report or something like that, and all of a sudden they slap their forehead and say, you know what, gosh, this is wrong; we shouldn't be doing this.

They themselves have to come to the conclusion that the cost-benefit calculus has changed, and the way you change that is you alter their view--until recently--which is that everything they were exfiltrating was absolutely true, and so I call this the "poison the well" strategy. In other words, the extent to which we begin using honey nets and other things, that they start exfiltrating bad data, and their bureaucracy has to spend more and more resources actually figuring out whether things are true or not, and they start getting bad information from below, a couple of things are going to happen naturally, particularly in China, where the government are such great control freaks.

The first thing that's going to happen is they're going to start arranging some circular firing squads at the local level, you know, who's the leak, who's the mole, where's the problem? And it's going to lead to a tendency that I think is absolutely critical, which is right now we have this bottom up, grassroots, entrepreneurial sort of cyber espionage framework as in complete contrast to our system, which is top down and tight sphinctered and controlled and everything else.

The more problems they have in that system will lead them to begin to accelerate the trends toward centralization of authority and decision-making. To be a little glib, I think the goal of our policy should be to make it as difficult to get a computer network exploit operation approved in the Chinese system as it is currently in our system.

But next to every Chinese 3PLA technical reconnaissance bureau operator, I want an auditor, I want a lawyer, and I want someone from the IG, just like in our system. And so that will reduce the tempo of the activity, and the leadership will have to weigh in on a much greater basis about the potential risks of that activity. It will go from being a Wild West go out and steal the data and develop the tools and then come tell us what you've found kind of system to one in which there's much greater input from above in terms of the risk calculus of engaging in that kind of activity.

So to summarize, I sort of have a hit them high, hit them low kind of strategy. Clearly we need to still have dialogue, and we still need to demarche them, and we still need to talk about arms control and cyber crime cooperation, and we need to deal with Internet governance issues, and all of that, but that to me is really not where we're going to get the traction.

We have to do all of that to maintain the posture. Where we're really going to get that traction is if we change the leadership's own view of the utility of this activity. The way to do that is to get them off the idea that this is ultra, that this is this fantastic intelligence collection program, and, in fact, that the gig is up, and that they need to alter that.

CHAIRMAN REINSCH: Bruce.

MR. QUINN: Well, Mr. Chairman, thank you very much for the invitation, and it's a pleasure to be here today, apparently as the only private company represented here today.

But let me just begin by saying that, first and foremost, Rockwell Automation is a happy partner, if you will, with our Chinese counterparts in China. We've been there for more than 30 years now, been very successful in that marketplace. We have invested. We have a policy around the world to try to control our intellectual property and technology so we've invested in wholly-owned enterprises, manufacturing enterprises in China.

We've acquired some companies there in China as well, and we work with our Chinese partners around the globe. So, again, I would stress that we are happy partners in working with the Chinese and we've been very successful in that marketplace, and we will continue to do that, I think.

Secondly, we view the cyber security issue as a global one, and so when we look at it as a company, we don't specifically think about a particular country targeting us. We don't have the ability to determine for ourselves where the attribution comes from. We only know that our system is being probed or looked at or something has been put into it possibly, and we have to investigate that.

I think my other point would be that from our point of view companies themselves, private companies in the U.S., probably have the burden of protecting their intellectual property themselves. Since our company came about, we've been protecting our intellectual property. Regardless of how that intellectual property is being stolen or that someone is trying to steal it, we've protected it from all means, not just cyber, but all means.

And so I think it's up to companies to identify for themselves, for example, what are the family jewels, what are we trying to protect, what makes us, what our differentiator is, and what makes us successful in the world versus our competition. We need to protect those most closely, and in doing that, we have to determine where a potential threat might be anywhere in the world, and do we want to forward move that intellectual property that's so important to us into that environment?

In our case, we probably don't want to do that, and we maintain that important intellectual property back in the United States, not to say that that can't still be broken into now, particularly with this new threat from cyber security.

So, again, our point of view, is that it's a global problem. We also feel that companies really do have the burden of protecting their intellectual property. I think where we want to turn to the government for assistance is, number one, information. We do need to level the playing field. We know that the U.S. government has significant resources that can assist us in, number one, identifying potential threats and letting us know where the greatest threats globally are to the theft of our intellectual property.

Secondly, if they've identified where those threats are coming from, they can also help us understand the technologies that those persons are using to try to steal our intellectual property; they can explain to us what some countermeasures might be that we can undertake within our company to best protect ourselves. So we get an idea of where the danger is at and then how to protect ourselves based on the government's best possible advice.

When I work overseas, and I, as a private citizen, go up to the U.S. Embassy, I've only got a couple of contacts that I can really go to. One of them is the Commercial Service at embassies, maybe in some countries it's going to be an Economic Officer that works on behalf of the Commercial Service. They provide things like, you know, giving people introductions to agents and distributors in the country. They are very necessary tasks, but it's also somewhat fluffy.

What would be nice is to also be able to get a briefing when you're at the embassy there on the potential threat that might be occurring to your company and to your intellectual property in that country. The U.S. government doesn't share that information within itself. So the Commercial Officer is not going to have access to what DoD has or to what NSA has or to whatever agency it is that has that data. That isn't even shared internally so then it can't be provided to us in a classified or non-classified environment.

So I think helping us level the playing field as much as possible will give us a great leg up at protecting our intellectual property.

I also think that this is a problem that companies need to manage. It's going to exist. The technology to attack us does outstrip our defenses and always will. We're not a government. We can't put defenses up so high that we can't do business. We have to still be able to do business with the public and with our customers, and so there's a level of defense that we can put up, and then there's a level we just can't go beyond.

But you can strategize about how to handle these things. Looking at each country individually, we can determine how best to protect that. For example, in China, one of the things I do is I take a look at the-- very simply speaking--I'm not going to get too technical here--I look at the Chinese Five Year Plan, and the Five Year Plan pretty much tells me what the Chinese are going to be focusing on. Part of that most recent Five Year Plan talks about how the Chinese would like to see greater innovation and investment in their industrial automation sector so I know that they want to become competitors. They would like to see a national champion, a Chinese national champion company rise up and compete with my company, Seimens, Schneider, etc., all the large multinational automation providers in the world.

So I know that's going to happen. China then identifies key national players to be those companies, and they put resources, R&D money, seed money, they incubate this company to become successful. Those companies then approach us directly and say, hey, we'd like to partner with you, hey, we'd like to buy your technology, we'd like to work with you, and that's one area that I can manage. I might just work with one of those rising national champions to be a partner with them, get to know them a little bit better.

The long and the short of it is that if there's going to be a leakage of our intellectual property, at the end of the day, it will come out and be visible to us through one of those national champions at the end of it, and then what do you have? You merely have a case of a private company or a state-owned enterprise, either one, that's now possibly stolen, if we've identified it's stolen, our intellectual property or there's a trademark violation.

And we can address it as we would any other trademark or intellectual property violation that we've found around the world, and we would do that through legal means and through the help of the U.S. government obviously, in the way that we would handle any trademark violation or stolen intellectual property violation that we found. So I guess that's how I would begin it. I'd certainly have other suggestions and ideas.

CHAIRMAN REINSCH: Okay. That's good. I want to at some point get back to Roy to talk about the Commission's recommendations, but both Mike and Dennis had a comment so go ahead.

COMMISSIONER WESSEL: I'd like to divide the question a little bit because, in part, James, what I heard you talking about is more governmental assets, and, Roy, your discussion I think, in part, is the private sector. And as the Commission, our job is to advise Congress on not only the scope of the problem--we're not going to talk about that here--but recommendations on solutions.

Talking to a lot of private sector enterprises, unless you're a

Rockwell or a major company, you may either not see yourself as a high value target or you're small enough that you're not going to expend the resources on perimeter defenses, et cetera. But you're also going to be scared to death about telling the public that your intellectual property has actually been stolen.

So, a couple of questions. What I heard you were talking about, James, was more about governmental assets because the cost is in that sense. Your Commission was focused, I believe, a lot more on the private sector and the hundreds of billions of dollars of IP that's being stolen.

How do you address the problem of the attribution in the sense of a company doesn't want to tell Wall Street that it's IP has been stolen because that's a huge hit on their stock? They often find out after the cat is out of the bag, et cetera. I found some of the recommendations of the Commission sort of trying to address it in a way that I don't think companies are actually going to back you up, if you will.

So, again, sort of real life private sector. Governmental assets I think are one tranche, but we're also talking about broader private sector issues.

MR. KAMPHAUSEN: A couple thoughts. I think you're exactly right. We've had a fair amount of pushback from companies, either individually or through associations, since the Commission report came out. And I would characterize them in a couple of ways. The first is let's avoid doing harm or, in the first instance, do no harm. Don't make a situation worse by the kinds of things that you recommend or that you advocate for on the Hill or in the administration, and the commissioners, I think, were very sensitive to that.

We also found that, though, in parallel, companies are, for the reason you talk about, unwilling or unable to speak to tell their own stories. So, in some respects, the Commission found itself advocating on behalf of a broad cross-section of sectors and companies who wouldn't necessarily associate themselves with the recommendations that the Commission came up with, and that's kind of a funny space to be in after the fact, then, when you talk about--

CHAIRMAN REINSCH: Wait a minute. They wouldn't publicly associate themselves with them or they don't agree with them privately?

MR. KAMPHAUSEN: They certainly wouldn't publicly associate. Because they were unwilling or unable to talk about the scope of their own problems to the extent that would have been most helpful, we ended up then advocating in positions that they wouldn't agree with even in private after the fact. That's kind of a funny space to be in.   That's one point.

The other point is the commissioners were very taken with the problem that you talk about, Mr. Wessel, and that it is that there are big companies that on scale suffer the most. But there are also small and medium-sized companies that relative to the size of their network suffer far more, and in many cases cease to exist. That's the part I don't think we were able to address as effectively as we had hoped we would have been able to.

In the recommendations, one of the things we did in response to that was to avoid putting in our cyber recommendations as a sort of laundry list of helpful things to do. In fact, we judged that would undermine the strength of the report and would, in fact, encourage people to think they could get by with the sort of passive vulnerability mitigation steps that James has said and the commissioners firmly believe just will not protect you in the end if you are a target.

So, you ought not have a false sense of security if you're a small or medium-sized enterprise, but then that appears to say, then, what the Commission is arguing is every firm needs to have a big cyber security consultant entity that advises it, and they certainly wouldn't agree with that as well.

But that then leads to a discussion of how you can use your own means to protect what is yours. And the commissioners were quite taken-- this gets to some of the follow-up recommendations--the commissioners were quite taken with the notion, albeit with caveats and questions, but they're quite taken with the notion that there ought to be some parallel understanding of legal protections afforded you in cyberspace as there are in the physical world.

In other words, if something is taken from you, you have certain rights pertaining to it. It doesn't cease to be yours when it has left your network, for instance, and so you ought to have some protections that you don't currently have, and there are a couple of ways that goes.

One is to say you can build in protections into a packet of information that you can then activate once it leaves your network, either disabling the information or in a more extreme case doing harm to the network that it finds itself in.

That's not legal currently, and the commissioners were well aware of that. They're arguing, though, that absent our movement to a discussion of what this changed environment means, some companies who have suffered great loss may say what's the harm in us taking matters into our own hands? We had some say that to us in effect.

So one has to proceed with due diligence with regard to civil liberty protection and privacy protections. I mean these are the kind of national figures that you would expect would be concerned about those sorts of things, but at the end of the day, they also said we ought to not be more concerned about the security and integrity of the network that has taken something from us than we are about the information and the network from which it was taken.

COMMISSIONER WESSEL: Let me operationalize it, and let's take this umbrella. Let's say that the expansion mechanism, whatever, the IP of that is key. The Chinese go into your computer, take the IP, the designs and everything else you were talking about, information qua information and not the fruits of that information, if you will. We have some remedies. 337 allows you to stop, you know, the fruit of the poisonous tree coming over here, but we've seen no willingness of the Chinese when we have asked them to. When we take evidence to them on the theft of our IP and how it's being used in their market, we've seen little evidence of their willingness to do it.

Understanding you have good relationships with China, have you utilized the legal system there, and what has been the product of that for you?

MR. KAMPHAUSEN: A couple thoughts. First, enormous strides have been made within the Chinese legal system with regard to protection of intellectual property and then enforcement actions once cases are brought.

Second, a very small proportion of the cases brought in Chinese courts are brought by international actors. They're almost all Chinese internal. And whether there's a degree of self-selection there or there's a sense that you're never going to get redress within the Chinese system, the reality is the percentage is very, very low. It could be higher, and actually according to the folks who talk with us, the likelihood of success is increasing if the merits of the case so warrant.

But I think the other part of that is it's a system that's reforming and getting better. The other part the Commission said is in the conduct of the report, its research and its writing, there is an intentional effort to focus it on American interests and speak to the American people and American leadership. In fact, the first sentence of the report says "we present this report to the American people for their consideration."

There's acknowledgement that there's huge impact, in effect, that's called for on the part of Chinese leadership and Chinese companies. There was an intentional effort to say that would take place in follow-on effort that we were not going to manage the outreach as part of the development of the report. So given particularly who the two co-chairs were, there was an understanding that you don't make progress in China just by naming and shaming and poking people in the eye, but that we would sequence those efforts, and that the first would focus on the delivery or the report itself.

CHAIRMAN REINSCH: Bruce, do you agree with what he said about companies there?

MR. QUINN: Well, I'll mention a couple of things. I think the first part of it was discussion between companies and the government and the reluctance on the part of companies to talk to the government. I completely agree. We've always had this problem. I was a diplomat in China for five years working on the commercial side, and then in a private company for another five years, and we've always had this problem.

Well, come to us and tell us about your trade issue. Come to us and tell how you're being hurt. And then they'll tell us about it in private, and then when you start to put it on a piece of paper, no, no, no, don't do that. So that is a problem, and so what I would say about that is that we really, ultimately, frankly, need to get to a point where the government is our doctor or our lawyer when it comes to sharing this type of information. I think if you look at the comments that all of the main business associations and organizations here in town, I would say that we support the Business Roundtable's position on the cybersecurity bill here in the United States, for example, and we have a position on that.

We need to come to that place where we can trust the government, and that's not only the government saying, yeah, they want a protected force, but then suddenly they're FOIAed, or there's another public access to that information. There needs to be a level of comfort between the companies and the government if we're going to be able to share that kind of information.

And I think it's critical to getting to this issue. I mean if we're not sharing information, we just have what we have, and best practices cannot be shared then. So that's one point.

I think as far as this commercialization of stolen intellectual property and the use of it in China and things like that, I would say, first and foremost, we've been very lucky. We have not been hit by this in China today. I think that has to do with the technology level of our products, the fact that our products do not tend to work individually or by themselves. They work within a system so it requires a long line of technologies that need to be developed. So it's not just knocking off one of our products, sticking into a factory system and making it work. That doesn't happen.

Also, I want to say something about the sophistication of our customers in China. Chinese companies today want to be world class. They want to be the most efficient. They want to make a product as fast and as cheaply as anyone else in the country. China is moving away from the business they did in the past, which is the low end assembly plant. They don't want to be that. They'd rather see that in Vietnam today or Cambodia or Malaysia or someplace else.

They want to be an advanced manufacturer. They're not going to purchase knocked-off, untested, cheap factory automation. So they're going to turn to legitimate suppliers for those things until one of their national champions has got their technology up to a particular level. And again, watching the rise of that national champion is where you're going to see any leakage of intellectual property, and then once you see that, at that level that national champion begins to utilize, let's say, leaked or taken stolen intellectual property, then you can effectively go after that. I agree with Roy that the IP courts, particularly in China, have really gotten better.

I mean it's not perfect yet, but certainly there has been a lot of effort on the part of the USG to work with these intellectual property courts. They're separate from the other court systems in China, and they have become more usable. I think when you do your contract, you always talk about offshore arbitration. That hasn't changed, but we have found that the courts have been citing more and more on behalf of foreigners in the country--not always. There are still problems, but again it has become a venue that you can turn to.

CHAIRMAN REINSCH: Dennis, do you want to come in?

VICE CHAIRMAN SHEA: Well, maybe my question will elicit more information about Roy's report, and I know you want to get there.

First of all, I want to congratulate the Commission on the report. I think it was a tremendous public service and, particularly, not only the focus, but the fact that you outlined a set of policy prescriptions. You've provided a menu of options for people in the Congress and the administration to consider.

Now with that said, you say the problem is about a $300 billion problem in very approximate terms. You agree with Keith Alexander that this is the greatest transfer of wealth in human history. Now that's a pretty big statement.

Then I'm going to read, Roy, from your report, because when I read it, I said "right on, this is exactly right." And you hinted at it in your opening remarks. You say the Commission regards changing the incentive structure for IP thieves to be the paramount goal in reducing the scale and scope of IP theft. Simply put, the conditions that encourage foreign companies to steal American intellectual property must be changed in large part by making theft unprofitable.

The starting point is the recognition that access to the American market is the single-most important goal of foreign firms seeking to be international corporate leaders. And basically you're saying that you have to make the costs exceed the benefits of engaging in this behavior. But then I read your policy responses to make the costs exceed the benefits. You talked about speeding up the 337 process, providing more resources for the FBI, and giving the Treasury the authority to exclude companies from the banking system--as if the Treasury is going to be very active in doing that--I just felt disappointed. I felt that the proposed responses to achieving your goal of making the costs exceed the benefits didn't really get there.

So, I'm wondering, tell me how I'm wrong. Or maybe there are other things you considered but ultimately didn't put in the report as a Commission recommendation.

MR. KAMPHAUSEN: I think it's a fair comment and observation. I have a couple responses. The first is the commissioners were mindful that there ought to be a kind of graduated series of responses to the problem, not exclusively to Chinese entities, although the commissioners judged that China is the origin of a large proportion of the problems that we face, but that it ought to be steps. So some of the recommendations are first steps. In fact, they phased them to occur over the short, medium and long-term. Even within each category, there are some that are more stringent and others that are more early stage recommendations. That's the first point.

You have to be mindful of the environment in which the recommendations are taking place. You have companies that are very successful--Bruce said, "lucky." I think it's maybe partly that and partly great management, but, in any case, you can't do harm to the whole system by immediately instituting the most stringent measures.

Then the commissioners said there are other things we could do, and in Chapter 14, as I'm sure you've read, are the things that they considered and ultimately did not recommend.

VICE CHAIRMAN SHEA: Slade Gorton.

MR. KAMPHAUSEN: And Slade, Senator Gorton's is in there as well.

The commissioners judged that if we accurately assess what is most desired by those rising, globally aspiring companies, we accurately judge that it is operating within the U.S. market and operating using the U.S. banking system, for instance, if you judge that right, its impact on behavior will be immediate and significant. If you think about the use of anti-terrorism finance, for instance, which is really the origin of the idea that we could use the banking system to deter illegal behavior, that's going to attempt to persist using alternative means.

Well, it's quite the contrary in this case. We have companies that want to operate and do so legally and make money in the process. The idea that they might somehow be listed and prevented from operating within the American market would have a huge preemptive deterrent effect, the commissioners judged. And so it will take a period of time, but I think they judged that we need to begin the process and then step up the pressure as they move along. And that's not entirely satisfying to you, I can tell, from the look on your face, but that's how they thought about it.

VICE CHAIRMAN SHEA: No, I mean you look at Iran sanctions. I'm not an expert on Iran sanctions, but there always seems to be an extreme effort on the part of the Administration to exclude, to make exceptions rather than to sanction companies, and Sinopec is a major player and a major player in selling refined petroleum to Iran, and they've never been, as I recall, sanctioned. So, again, your report was such a valuable document because whether people agree or disagree with individual elements of it, you actually attempted to lay out a policy response. So I thought it was extremely helpful in that regard.

CHAIRMAN REINSCH: I want to--do you want to add something, James, and then I--

DR. MULVENON: Well, just a couple of reactions to what we've been talking about. My company, I actually was appointed the CIO and CSO of my company because I was the only person who gave a damn, and the COO wrapped his arm around me and said it's only a small reduction in salary.

And I extensively share information with the U.S. government. I have a deep and abiding and a long-term relationship with the FBI. Now, admittedly, I'm a small company, we're not publicly traded, and I don't have seven layers of lawyers sitting on top of me. The boss just said share what you need to share, and I also exist within a classified defense contractor framework that affords me certain protections and gives me certain channels for getting data that other people don't have.

But what I consistently hear from companies is very similar to what Mr. Quinn is saying in the sense that they want, they want some signal from Congress, and I think the Commission, when I testified before the Commission in sunny Seattle, we talked about this at length, they want some sort of indemnification that says if we share information with the U.S. government, that that will then not result in some sort of an SEC problem or some sort of DOJ problem because we've now shown that we've had some loss in shareholder value that is going to have some impact upon us.

And that's the thing, that's one thing that I've been looking for on the congressional side that I have not seen.

COMMISSIONER WESSEL: But let me ask a question here. I apologize for interrupting. And I agree with you, but how do you then take that to the operational side? The umbrella guy--

DR. MULVENON: Right.

CHAIRMAN WESSEL: --goes to the federal government, the government says okay, thanks for sharing, we're going to go do something about it. They go to the Chinese and say you're stealing this, the Chinese say no, what's--

DR. MULVENON: Well, I mean I do believe in strategic naming and shaming in the following sense, which is to say--

COMMISSIONER WESSEL: But then that company is outed.

DR. MULVENON: Right. But the more important point is--I'm not even concerned about that one company--but we need to create a constituency of people in China who want to succeed but are being harmed by government cyber espionage efforts that they had nothing to do with.

In other words, the companies and the civilian universities that I could name today that are known players in the cyber espionage, either as contractors to the military or the state security apparatus or are building the malware and the tools that are being used by those guys, the extent to which they get on a denied entities list, and they can't get visas, and those professors can't get fellowships, and they can't come to the United States, again, this is about changing the cost-benefit calculus on the Chinese side rather than some sort of gaiatsu from the outside that is exogenously trying to hector them about it.

It's only--you know, we always say, and I believe there is a lot of truth to it, that the Chinese will begin to protect intellectual property when they have intellectual property to protect; right? And this behavior will only be curbed when there is a constituency within China that is feeling the pain of what other people are doing.

Now, you have to be strategic about it. It's very likely that very large state enterprises in China have been direct beneficiaries of some of this information, the Sinopecs, the Sinochems, the people on that scale. The level of interdependence that those companies have with foreign multinationals in deals right now would be self-defeating in some cases to go after those guys, and this has been an intense topic of discussion within our government about whether to go down that road.

We also need to make one following distinction that we haven't made today that I think is absolutely critical. I divide commercial espionage into two basic buckets, one which is sensitive business information, which is you break into a major multinational oil company's c-suite e-mail, you find their bid price on a tract underneath the water in the South China Sea, and the Chinese company comes in $100 less, and they win the bid; right? That's immediately actionable.

What I'm less confident about is this chain of custody on stealing IP, and I agree with Mr. Quinn about highly complex stuff, but even simpler stuff, even source code, you know, because of the lack of U.S. company disclosures, it's been very difficult for us to be able to identify a number of use cases where something was stolen via cyber espionage, it was allocated to a designated national champion in China, who then reverse engineered it successfully, was then able to productize it, marketize it, and then show a calculable loss of U.S. company market share in China and then loss of market share globally.

And I do believe that this push since 2006 for indigenous innovation, which I really think is frankly coterminous with where we saw the Chinese intrusion sets start going after commercial targets, and as an intelligence officer, I don't believe in coincidences, it's still not clear to me that state-driven R&D is not an oxymoron on the level of jumbo shrimp or military intelligence, and despite my Irish heritage, the only good news that I have coming to this story is that the Chinese have not shown me yet that they are capable of stealing highly complex advanced technology, reverse engineering it, and getting even the first generation's benefit from it, and then I'm even more skeptical that they could then continue to innovate beyond that since they didn't develop the technology organically within their system, and which would then likely have to lead them to steal the next generation after that.

And so most of my focus has been with companies is, you know, continue to maintain your own innovative R&D here, protect the crown jewels, and then seek remedy in specific cases where you know that particular naming and shaming would build that constituency inside China that would have the desired long-term effect.

CHAIRMAN REINSCH: There are several threads that I think are worth unraveling a little bit more, and I want to mention three of them and then pursue one of them. One is the issue of government, U.S. government-private sector cooperation. I have a thought about that I want to share with you.

The second one is how you actually implement something. Naming and shaming is easy to implement -- you name and hope they're shamed -- but if there's going to be, as was recommended, some kind of action, some kind of sanction attached to the naming, then you get into a whole host of implementation questions like the criteria used for doing that, and there are sufficiency questions and things that I think we ought to spend a few minutes on.

The third thread that I want to come back to probably last is one that Dennis raised in his reference to Iran, which is an area where I've done a lot of work wearing my other hat, which is that our policy there is a reflection of the fact that we have a multilateral problem, not a unilateral problem.

And it's related to how do we build multilateral support for what we want to do? I would argue this is a multilateral problem, too. We are not the only people that are victims here, and the Chinese are not the only people that are engaging in the activity. What are the implications? Every time we do something unilateral, there are other implications. How do we or should we try to multilateralize this problem? And if so, how do we do that?

But that's the third thread, and I hope we can pursue it. We have plenty of time to pursue all three of them.

Let me come back to the first one, on cooperation, and ultimately ask a question, but tell a story. One of the projects that I've been involved in, again, wearing another hat, is an effort to promote information sharing between private companies and the government on export control related and technology transfer related issues, the theory being from a government perspective that companies like Bruce's company have access to lots of information that would actually be useful to the American intelligence community.

Mostly this is information in the nature of inquiries about products, inquiries about systems, coming from places that you know you will not be allowed to sell to, and so that information is simply deleted, removed, or thrown away and not responded to often.

From an intelligence perspective, that's information that actually could be very useful because it would help intelligence people, if they are doing it with a lot of companies, pick up patterns and networks that they might not have seen individually, and it also allows them to uncover either new people that have entered this universe or old people that have renamed themselves as somebody else and relocated themselves with a different address.

All of this is useful, yet this kind of information sharing is not taking place, so we embarked on an effort to see if we could do that, and what we discovered was a variation of what you're talking about, that basically the feds come in, talk to a company about this, and the first thing the company says is let me have you talk to my general counsel, and the first thing the general counsel says is, you know, we're not against this, this is a good idea. We're a patriotic company, we want to make sure we don't end up as part of an enforcement investigation, and we don't want to end up in a voluntary disclosure trap and a variety of penalties.

Can you, FBI, assure us--or not the FBI--can you, the Justice Department, assure us that that's not going to happen if we cooperate? And the answer to that question is invariably no. We want you to cooperate, and then you take your chances. Now let me ask our experts there, is it possible to get over that hump?

DR. MULVENON: Again, I just want to emphasize that there's a distinction. I think that there has been a tremendous amount of success on that side, on the defense industry side, and for obvious reasons, but I want to highlight specifically what happened was, you know, when Deputy Secretary Lynn introduced the Defense Industry pilot, the DIB, everyone from the outside thought, oh, well, the benefit of this is we're going to get classified threat signatures from NSA.

That wasn't the secret. The secret was the wink and the nudge from DoD that said go ahead and collude with each other and share information with each other about the threats you see in your own network, and we're not going to penalize you for engaging in that kind of behavior, and DOJ is not going to get involved, and there is no antitrust implications and everything else.

That was the real secret. Now, the question has always been, and I've been working on this as well, is how do you translate that kind of a framework outside of the defense industrial system, which has its own protections, and your ability to share that information?

CHAIRMAN REINSCH: It's a world of its own.

DR. MULVENON: Yeah, it is, and how do you encourage collective action at that level? And I'm beginning to see some of that. The one thing that the Commission and I talked about, which is sort of once you engage in collective action, there's another tendency that arises that also requires congressional remedy, which is the rise of certain companies, who will remain unnamed, who are making promises to Fortune 500 companies that they will, in fact, on your behalf engage in active defenses or hack back or go and get your data or actively run offensive counterintelligence operations within your network and help you build deception systems and things like that so that the document that gets exfiltrated has metadata in it that will beacon and will tell you where it is and everything else.

And that is a legal gray area right now that is frankly not well covered by the 1986 Computer Fraud and Abuse Act, which is horribly out of date and needs to be updated, and a lot of the interesting discussion with the Commission was related to that. I mean General Hayden has said publicly that unless companies have a greater confidence that the government can help them, that he expects the rise of digital "Blackwaters," of companies that are going to go out as mercenaries and do this on your behalf.

That is not in the interest of the U.S. government. It's not even in the interest of U.S. companies to get into that kind of a framework because what will happen is companies will get themselves in trouble, and then they will turn to the government and say this is now a national security issue because we tangled with the wrong group of hombres; now, you need to come in and help us.

And so companies are then putting the U.S. government in situations that they don't want to be in, and that are highly uncomfortable, and so that really demands on the front end that we fix that problem, and we have much better bright line distinctions in those laws about where the boundary lines are, what are you allowed to do, and what are you not allowed to do in terms of going after your data and understanding where it went?

You know this device I'm holding, you know, if someone stole this, we have apps on here that allow me to then figure out where it went. It will take a picture of the person if they're holding it in front of their face. It will tell me their geolocation, all of that, because I owned it; right? And I can shut it down, wipe it remotely because I was the owner of it, and similar type of thinking needs to be done about other pieces of intellectual property that get stolen and what exactly are our rights, and that is absolutely unclear right now under the law.

CHAIRMAN REINSCH: Roy and Bruce, do you want to comment on that?

MR. KAMPHAUSEN: You know earlier Bruce said companies need to manage their own problems; they need to do their own risk mitigation. I don't know if I'm quoting you exactly, but the point is well taken, and I think the Commission would say we absolutely agree. But companies also need the right tools that afford them the protections, legal and otherwise, so that they can do what's in their own interest, and this is a very thin eyr of a needle that needs to be thread because, on the one hand, companies want the protections to make their own decisions that are in their own best interests.

On the other, the government has to be concerned about the development of, as James said, a Wild West scenario where everyone does what's right within their own eyes. One of the thoughts is to say the technology is not mature enough yet to allow us to talk about securing our own information once it's left our network. So let's just focus exclusively at the information-sharing level for a period of time.

The other point of view says the technology will develop along the lines that law and policy guide it, and it seems to me that's an area where the Commission can have an effect on the Congress because at the moment the Congress is really not clear on how it wants to develop its thinking and the legislation that it wants to see passed.

So the Commission would say we don't know the exact solution, but we know that the path to the solution has got to be made up of industry, policy, staff, and it's got to be one that proceeds very carefully.

Related to that, the Commission is really in favor and strongly supports the development by Executive Order of a lead Cabinet official who will manage all aspects of IP protection, and the Commission said it ought to be the Secretary of Commerce, and those who come from a trade background almost uniformly say that's a bad call.

[Laughter.]

MR. KAMPHAUSEN: It's a weak entity.

CHAIRMAN REINSCH: Now wait a minute.

[Laughter.]

CHAIRMAN REINSCH: Go ahead.

MR. KAMPHAUSEN: It's striking--

COMMISSIONER WESSEL: The experts agree with you.

CHAIRMAN REINSCH: People with experience. Go ahead.

MR. KAMPHAUSEN: What's interesting about it is the alternatives are unknown, and frankly the commissioners are pretty cognizant of how U.S. interagency functions, and USTR is not in a position to manage the integration of the entire U.S. government to respond to these sorts of problems. It's externally focused, doesn't have enough staff, arms, and legs to make things happen.

So, as a function of capabilities, the commissioners judged that the Secretary of Commerce should be the person, and the argument then we've not had a lot of really ambitious and successful Secretaries, frankly, is not a sufficient one for saying that's not a reason to try it. But you may not agree with that. You may not agree with the person or the entity, but it seems clear that the identification of that senior administration official needs to be done so that we can manage an effective interagency process and response.

CHAIRMAN REINSCH: Bruce, you want to comment, and then Mike has something.

MR. QUINN: Yeah, just briefly. I think what both these gentlemen have just mentioned, I would agree with it. I think that is the big hurdle, you know. Companies right now want to be patriotic. We're a patriotic company obviously, just as you said. But there is real ramifications to sharing information, and a company will look at it and say, well, where's the upside for us? What are we getting in return for this?

And I think it's not two-way right now. It's please provide us information; we'll get back to you. There is no, there is no window for us to step forward to the government except for agencies that both might regulate and later take action against us. That's the only agencies we have access to. That's why it's scary. What we'd rather work with is a window organization or agency within the government that would be more two-way to us.

It isn't the SEC or the FBI or someone like that who we know could come back to us because we've disclosed just the wrong thing for some reason. Rather, we would be working with a more operational agency, if you will, or conglomerate that could provide information back to us. It would be a two-way street. We're going to provide you this information, and then because of that, we're going to provide you a report back that says what we've found out through our sources, our methods, of where this stands at.

CHAIRMAN REINSCH: I should have said in the story I was telling that the project in question envisioned exactly that, and envisioned not only the private companies have information that would be of interest to the federal government, the government has information that would be of interest to companies. That seemed to be less of a problem from the government's standpoint, although different people have different views about that, but the problem of having appropriate legal protections turned out to be--well, this is not done yet, but so far it's been insoluable.

It also produced the same discussion that the Commission had about who should be doing this, and just without getting into the weeds of agencies, what we discovered was that the people in the United States government that would be the recipients of the information the private parties would provide did not have any particular interest in receiving that information directly, and the companies didn't have any particular interest in providing that information directly.

And so the one area where there did seem to be common agreement was there needed to be an interface, and it needed to be a commercial interface rather than an intelligence interface. So we ended up in the Department of Commerce, as well, not because of any inherent strength or weakness in the department, but because neither the intelligence people nor the companies wanted to talk to each other directly for a variety of reasons, and so is there a third party that could be both the funnel and the filter?

Anyway, Mike.

COMMISSIONER WESSEL: Going back to springboard off of Dennis' comments about the report, and I think the number is $338 billion a year, I think was the amount that's being stolen, and the question of scope. In a time of sequester, can our government really do this?

A CEO of a small company recently called me because they had found out that they were a victim of intrusions, asked me for some advice. I called a friend in law enforcement. They said we may be able to sit down privately as a favor, but we don't do this normally. I mean maybe if you're a cleared defense contractor, you got it, but otherwise you can't.

Commerce is having its budget cut. Everyone is having its budget cut. Not everyone can afford to hire a Mandiant or any of the others. Can we really get ahead of this? Should we take--and I apologize, I don't remember who talked about the 12th Five Year Plan--should we focus on what China is focusing on by, if you will, reverse engineering their 12th Five Year Plan and then having some cooperation between the public-private sector so that, and probably have to have some private sector resources, to really get ahead of this problem or focus?

CHAIRMAN REINSCH: Comments?

MR. KAMPHAUSEN: Well, the Under Secretary of Commerce and Director of the Patent and Trademark Office leads an organization that's fully fee-funded, and the most recent director, David Kappos, instituted the largest fee increase in the history of the organization. It's flush with cash.

COMMISSIONER WESSEL: It is also--also, it's months behind in terms of clearing anything, if not years.

MR. KAMPHAUSEN: And as I understand it, though it's a sequester-free organization, it's been obligated to comply with general constraints that other organizations, which are governed by the sequester, have to be concerned with.

So the point is to say not every entity is so grievously affected by sequester that no action can be taken.

The other argument for Commerce is it's just got all these pieces that if properly organized, managed and led could be much more successful, and the USPTO is one of them.

The notion--this is highly speculative--but the notion that we could sort of undertake a public-private study session of the implications of the Five Year Plan and then develop strategies in response, I mean that really leans itself, if not almost outright becomes, kind of sanctioned industrial policy. It doesn't have to be that way, but it sort of leans in that direction, and I think that's an entirely appropriate discussion to have.

We say the words, and red flags go up all over the place, but the concern about an excessively heightened degree of public-private information sharing is that it leads us in that direction. Maybe that's the necessary and only response. But I think we ought to be aware of those consequences going forward even though the Commission was wholeheartedly supportive of the kind of information sharing that Bruce talked about today.

CHAIRMAN REINSCH: Do you want to add anything, James?

DR. MULVENON: Well, it's interesting. One of our international partners, who will remain nameless, actually has had a strategy over the last two years of identifying three or four areas that they wanted to succeed in the bilateral trade relationship, individual sectors, and then went to the Chinese and said we want to cooperate with you in these sectors for mutual benefit, and we will be monitoring your cyber espionage against us in these sectors as evidence of goodwill.

And they've had mixed success, and because there are some initial benefits obviously for bilateral cooperation on some of these things, and even if your long-term strategy is to displace the country and the companies that you're working with.

But their analysis was based on exploitation of the 12th Five Year Plan and the 2006 to 2020 Mid-to-Long-Range Plan, and other things that people have written about extensively.

I was just at a meeting yesterday morning, internally, about Chinese S&T priorities, and there were probably 40 people in the room who look at this issue extensively within the intelligence community, and I can guarantee you there wasn't a single person in the room who even knew where to find the 12th Five Year Plan, much less having actually extracted the information from it about what China's priorities were, and that's been a real disconnect, and that's really troubling because, as I've often said about the Chinese, they say the damndest things in plain text.

I mean it's literally there for the reading. There is no secret about what the major industrial priority areas are that they're pursuing. It's not secret what the priorities of the 863 program are, and you can draw a direct thread, as Mr. Quinn did, between those things and the stand-up of national champions and decisions by the National Reform and Development Commission and specific policy documents that come out.

Now, admittedly, some of these policy documents are kept in the vest pocket and are never published and are sort of secret codicils within the State Council and other things. But, you know, China regards its language as its first line of national defense. It's its first layer of crypto.

[Laughter.]

DR. MULVENON: And most, if not all, of what we need to understand where their priorities are come from those documents, and those are the requirements documents that are driving the cyber espionage. So that is a breakdown in our system to not connect those dots.

CHAIRMAN REINSCH: Okay. Bruce, you want to comment? And then we'll go to Dennis.

MR. QUINN: Yeah. Just quickly, I would say that again when you look at a Five Year Plan, remember, that we use it. I did mention that I would look at it defensively, if you will, from that point of view, but really to a greater extent, I look at it from an opportunity standpoint. I look at that each time it comes out. I look at the R&D program that they have in place, and I say, well, heck, how can I make a buck here?

How can I align both the way that we talk about our products and the way that we operate in that country to align ourselves both verbally, as well as with action, in line with that Five Year Plan? That way when I go out to the provinces or I go to state-owned enterprises, I use the same buzzword. Sometimes I use it in Chinese so that they know that when they partner with me to do that business, that they're checking off one of their blocks, one of their PADR blocks, their evaluation blocks, by having done this particular item that my company, I'm showing how my product meets that need for them in that particular area.

And so hopefully I'm delaying and/or offsetting them having to go after that some other way, and also at the same time successfully making a sale on something. So--

CHAIRMAN REINSCH: Dennis.

VICE CHAIRMAN SHEA: I'd just make the observation first that the Mandiant Report says that the PLA Unit 61398 was focused on four of the seven strategic emerging industries in the Five Year Plan so that just sort of validates what's been said.

This is, I guess, for Roy. Did the Commission in laying out its proposed policy responses, did it consider that if U.S. government took action on these responses, it would not occur in a vacuum? Even if done on a multilateral basis, if you start sanctioning companies, if you start prosecuting certain individuals, there's going to be a Chinese response. Most likely, Chinese sanctions of U.S. companies, maybe Chinese prosecutions of U.S. individuals. I mean how did that, was that a consideration, and if so, how did it work into your--

CHAIRMAN REINSCH: Great question because that moves us on to the second thread I wanted to pursue, so perfect.

MR. KAMPHAUSEN: Well, I'm glad you raised it as well. So a couple of different ways to think about it. The first was given their backgrounds and the experiences that they've had, the commissioners are well aware that in this, as in many other domains, the most effective action is multilateral, and early on, they had an internal debate as to whether that process ought to begin and exist at the same time as the Commission's work was undertaken, and they judged that ought to also be sequenced to a later point. And an update on that in a minute.

And so there's a sense that this is the beginning of a process. It's not a fully formed package that's being delivered, but they also judge that we have to think about the problem for ourselves first, and they're cognizant of, aware of, concerned about the kinds of retaliation that companies might suffer for U.S. government policy, even companies that aren't related to a particular instance, and there are many examples that we can think of in that regard.

But they also judge that the specter of doing nothing means we live in at some level in a kind of coercive environment that ought not be sustained, and so again they're cognizant of the costs and want to do no harm, but also judge that doing nothing is perhaps worse than that.

Now, if you're an individual company that suffers, that's not a very good answer; right?

VICE CHAIRMAN SHEA: Right.

MR. KAMPHAUSEN: And I think that they understand that, and so there would be other remedies that would have to be undertaken, and that's really what calls for the multilateral response.

One last thing. One of the interesting feedbacks from the commercial sector we've heard is thinking about how to multilateralize via an international information-sharing effort known bad players, and whether it's a public list or a private list, you know, is still being conceived of and thought about, but the idea that if there was a framework in which companies could share that kind of information internationally, that might--with friends and allies, like-minded partners--that that might be a first step along that way.

VICE CHAIRMAN SHEA: So there's a sense that if you took action, it would be a rocky road ahead, but ultimately the cost of doing nothing is unacceptable, and there's a recognition that the national interest is more important, supersedes maybe the collection of individual interests that might be affected; is that fair to say?

CHAIRMAN REINSCH: James.

DR. MULVENON: The question is who multilaterally; right?

VICE CHAIRMAN SHEA: Yes.

DR. MULVENON: And I will say, and this obviously reflects my own parochial interest, where we've had the most success, again, because of this nexus where you have the commercial aspects of the cyber espionage question overlaid on the government's interests and the internal interests about the cyber espionage, you know, because the Chinese are not seeing the cute distinction that we're trying to make between commercial and noncommercial espionage for the simple reason that, on their side, the same actors are doing both.

So we continue to push this line, and we continue to argue to them, well, we're statutorily precluded from doing commercial espionage, and we'd have no practical way to distribute the results and everything else, and I made this argument to the Chinese over and over and over again in the kicker dialogue, and they just don't believe it.

You know, they just absolutely do not believe it. And so we continue to make that distinction, but given that, in fact, on the Chinese side that it's being done by the same actors means that it overlaps with a lot of U.S. government interests on the intelligence side, in particular. We've had remarkably good success at the Five Eyes level on multilateralizing it--even unclassified information--because of those trust relationships.

Where we've had less success is with the Europeans, and that is I think principally because of the competitive dynamic that's going on, and the Sturm und Drang that we currently feel on the Free Trade Agreement and all the other issues that are being inserted into that right now.

And so the people inside the system I deal with think of it as concentric circles, circles of trust, and we're trying to get the Five Eyes level cooperation right because it's the easiest, and we can do it the most securely. Beyond that would be the Europeans and others, and then there's a whole range of international actors, but we wanted to sort of work on that model in a smaller circle first.

CHAIRMAN REINSCH: Commissioner Wessel.

COMMISSIONER WESSEL: Two quick questions. One, when you were doing your hearings and all of your meetings, WIPO and some of the other international organizations, did you talk to them? Have you had discussions about, and WIPO, I guess, is more on the copyright base arena, as to what's going on?

Two, we have two big negotiations going on right now, the Trans-Pacific Partnership and now the TTIP, the Transatlantic. Do you think that putting something in there for cooperation might advance our economic interests as well, that maybe that's a venue for some type of work?

MR. KAMPHAUSEN: No direct interaction with WIPO. We had a briefing by a representative of the International Chamber of Commerce, but nothing direct beyond that with WIPO.

On your second point, I think the commissioners thought this was a likely and necessary next step, that TTP and TTIP were appropriate venues to raise the standards for the protection of intellectual property, and I think they would say to broaden the dimensions of cooperation and sharing.

CHAIRMAN REINSCH: I would say that having just spent a good bit of time with Europeans the last couple days since we're mobbed with them right now, this is a huge issue because of the recent events that James referred to. Yes. Well, it's still going on. I can testify to that personally. They're very agitated.

COMMISSIONER WESSEL: Shocked.

CHAIRMAN REINSCH: . It will manifest itself in the TTIP negotiations in the context of the debate over privacy because that's the issue that is on the table, and which will then spill over into digital trade and free flows of information. It's not a discussion that deals directly with intrusions because that's a national security issue, which is technically in the competence of the member states, not in the competence of the Commission.

On the other hand, if you're going to talk about rules for data sharing and rules for privacy, you end up talking about all the same things. So I think that's where it's going to come out.

Let me ask a question, particularly for Roy, but for anybody. And this picks up on the thread that we were just talking about. If you're going to embark on a program where the United States government identifies--and the question really is what that term is going to mean-- identifies somebody who has done something bad, if they've stolen somebody's IP, let's say, and leave aside how you know that, or if they got it from Bruce, or you discovered it on your own, and you decide you want to, per the Commission's recommendations, you want to take some sort of punitive action--it doesn't matter what it is--the question I have is what is your basis for making that decision?

What is the evidentiary basis that you have to have to decide that something is sanction worthy? We're a rule of law country, unlike the Chinese, and we have processes. We have 337. We have all these different things that require a lot of fact-finding and require an evidentiary process and some contention where the other guys, if they want to, can come in and say, no, no, no, it didn't happen that way, and then a decision-making process that is reasonably transparent and somebody decides at the end. How do you operationalize what you're recommending within that kind of framework, or do you not do it within that kind of framework?

MR. KAMPHAUSEN: I think you have to do it within that framework, and the Commission talked about this to some extent, though did not make formal recommendations on it.

But I guess there's a couple ways to think of it. The first is what the original source of the information would be?. Either it could be commercial in origin, except that's not going to happen unless we have the kind of information-sharing arrangements that provide the kind of protections that Bruce was talking about. But that could be a source. It could also be a U.S. government source, and we can imagine the kinds of things how that could occur.

And then in the Commission's thinking, it gets fed into a robust, lean, well-led, well-managed interagency group that triages the information and has developed a series of tests against which the information would be applied to see if it constitutes a violation. Then at a certain point, the Commission said it's probably not the first one, but at a certain point then--

CHAIRMAN REINSCH: A violation of what? U.S. law? Is that's what's being violated?

MR. KAMPHAUSEN: Yes, yes. Now, the test could be subjective. You could have information that was gained through non-public means. And the assessment of it then leads to a judgment that intellectual property has been stolen.

You could also have an objective test, which is to say these international companies lost in a court of law, and they lost two, three, four, five, whatever the number of times is. At a certain point, they are by virtue of that objective record entered on to a list. That's an easier test to apply. It's going to affect a lot fewer companies, and it's not clear the deterrent value that would have.

So it seems a thing, and the Commission did not make a judgment on this--this is me speaking kind in the follow-up discussions that occurred thereafter--it seems that some mix of objective and subjective would be the most appropriate.

But then you've got to allow for this response by the entity that would be affected, and I'm intentionally not using legal terms because it's probably not going to be within a court of law. I mean it could be, but we already have those mechanisms. So how that occurs and a company is able to represent itself or an entity is able to represent itself is important to be thought through, but that occurs at a later point.

CHAIRMAN REINSCH: But doesn't the attribution problem come back to bite you at this point? How do you really know that whoever it is that you've decided is a bad guy is the bad guy?

MR. KAMPHAUSEN: Right. Or if you know it very clearly, but you can't share the means by which you got it, that's problematical, to be sure.

DR. MULVENON: And not only that, but the timing. In other words, do we wait? Because my new book, Chinese Industrial Espionage, we were going over covers that we wanted to have, and I proposed a cover to the publisher, which was a picture from a Chinese company Web site of a vacuum cleaner that was the spitting image of one of these Dyson vacuum cleaners. They even used the same PANTONE colors that Dyson uses for the plastics--right--and the publisher wouldn't let me put it on the cover because they said they feared legal liability from making this accusation against this other company.

But if you wait in the process until the copycat Dyson vacuum cleaner shows up on the market, and you lose market share because they've undercut your price by 50 percent or whatever, are we simply slamming the barn door on this issue? In other words, the U.S. company will go out of business, but we've made this principled stand. Or do you lean further forward in a sort of Rumsfeldian sense, and do you say, well, maybe we'll accept a lower standard because we actually want to save this industry?

We don't want to sort of write an autopsy on this industry, but we actually want to save this industry. That to me is the delicate balance to deal with because then you may, in fact, accept a lower evidentiary standard. What may hang in the balance is the actual future of that industry, green tech being a perfect example, solar cells.

COMMISSIONER WESSEL: But you also may have to change our trade laws or other laws because we have a high injury standard. Not only do you have to show that your information, your IP, was stolen. Under some scenarios, you have to show that you were materially injured.

DR. MULVENON: Right.

COMMISSIONER WESSEL: Which means you get farther upstream, you can't stop it before it happens. How do you, in fact, check that maybe the product is not coming into the U.S., but it's being sold in a province in a China, you know? You're 20 miles away from the barn when the barn door is closed.

DR. MULVENON: Yes.

COMMISSIONER WESSEL: And there is no way at that point ability to get any kind of recompense.

CHAIRMAN REINSCH: Go ahead.

MR. KAMPHAUSEN: If I could, Mr. Chairman, one of the recommendations that has met no opposition is the recommendation that the Economic Espionage Act be amended to allow for a private right of action for an injured party. And this essentially means you can bring your own suit. You don't have to wait for the government to take one up on your behalf.

It would certainly increase caseload. There would be a body of law that would exist over time. And there's a sense you can actually get some recompense at an earlier point.

In parallel to that, the Commission then argued that the court of appeal for all Economic Espionage Act cases ought to be the Court of Appeal for the Federal Circuit, Judge Rader's court, and we had a fair amount of interaction with the Court in the process of coming up with this recommendation. They actually think it would have a lot of effect, both domestically and perhaps internationally as well.

CHAIRMAN REINSCH: As you pointed out, there are existing mechanisms. There's a case I was following for awhile in California of a small company that sued a very large Chinese company for incorporating its software code into its product. They sued them for I think $3 billion based on the number of copies that had been sold, which I thought was brilliant, and it was to me a very telling exercise because it seemed to me the evidence was very clear.

Unfortunately, well, maybe not unfortunately, the case got settled, and the terms are confidential. So I don't know what the outcome was, but it would be interesting because it seemed to me it was a very promising tool.

We did get a question that I want to ask because I think it's relevant to some of this discussion. I think maybe I'll ask Dr. Mulvenon, and then the others can comment if you want. Then I want to come back to the multi-country issue because we haven't, I think, entirely disposed of that.

The question is consider the small high-tech defense contractor that specializes in a critical technology that provides our Armed Forces with essential capabilities. If that firm is getting hacked by the Chinese, by the PLA, they lack the resources to defend themselves 24/7. Given the resources that the PRC can throw at them, how can the Defense Department help them defend their technology? Or are we immobilized due to ideological opposition to an IP industrial policy?

DR. MULVENON: Well, as an example, for instance, it's been publicly discussed that there's an issue with Lockheed Martin and the F-35 and the Chinese intrusions. In fact, because of the nature of those kinds of programs, a very close relationship with AT&L and the Pentagon and other people who are very focused then on monitoring what the Chinese might have exfiltrated, trying to identify from Chinese technical writings and other materials the extent to which the technology that the Chinese have developed a countermeasure to it, for instance. Or they have figured out a way to fine-tune their electronic warfare systems to deal with the synthetic aperture radar of that airplane.

And then use that information to then feed back through the classified acquisition channels, which is to say make the following modifications to the system, and then continue to monitor the Chinese materials to see if they come up with a counter to the counter.

That is possible because of the nature of the acquisition process within the Department. I've often said that one of the greatest enemies to American cybersecurity is the Federal Acquisition Regulations. In this case, that system works reasonably well, but it is predicated on having really good information about how it's been exploited potentially. That involves a lot of very meticulous exploitation of Chinese technical writings to be able to figure out--and, again, often discussed in the clear, in Chinese, by numbered research institutes and factories that work on those issues and published in Chinese journals because they correctly perceive that we do not have the linguistic capacity to exploit all that material.

While I'm thinking about it, there was one other issue that it seems to me is a rising problem that is a bank shot of the issues we've been discussing, which is the hacking that has gone into the Patent and Trademark Office. This has, in many ways, facilitated the rise of an incredible increase on the Chinese side of patent trolling, which is a form of intellectual property theft. If someone steals your PTO information on a particular technology and then tries to register that patent and trademark inside a Chinese system, that is as damaging, in my view, to a U.S. company's ability to work in that market as if they stole it and then reverse engineered the product and tried to sell it in competition with your product.

Because they can then get legal remedy from Chinese courts, and it's another cyber-enabled IP theft that I see a lot more evidence of, particularly if you do as I do, which is trolling cnpatent.com and other Web sites where you see Chinese putting up patents that give them broad ability to then sue U.S. companies.

CHAIRMAN REINSCH: So you're a troll, too?

DR. MULVENON: Yes, I am.

[Laughter.]

CHAIRMAN REINSCH: Mr. Kamphausen and then Commissioner Wessel.

MR. KAMPHAUSEN: Even those folks who argue for the improvements within the Chinese intellectual property legal system, even those who say they've made a lot of progress, regard this issue, the issue of petty patents, as being the most egregious aspect of the Chinese system. It has to be changed.

And the Commission while not trying to be too tutorial in tone essentially says in the report the Chinese need to end this system. It's beneath them and what they hope to become, and it just needs to be ended as quickly as possible.

CHAIRMAN REINSCH: Commissioner Wessel.

COMMISSIONER WESSEL: I wanted to go back to the question you asked on behalf of one of the people, because I don't know that you answered it in the sense that you were talking about defense policy, defense capabilities, and needing to go back, finding out what they've stolen and then countermeasures, et cetera, what is the small company do?

What should they be able to expect, if anything, from the federal government in terms of assistance? I know DSS and others supply some help. Or are they pretty much on their own?

DR. MULVENON: No, they're not. I mean I think that while it's not perfect, the defense-industrial base, of which I am a minor member, is actually the exemplar of the system working at its best. But it's entirely because, and not to repeat myself, DSS and other actors allow us to share information in a secure way that is protected from the kinds of possible SEC and DOJ sanction that a commercial company would not, and it's entirely because of the classification.

CHAIRMAN REINSCH: Okay. Let me suggest, unless anyone wants to add anything right at this point, let's return to an element of the third thread that I suggested, if we can, which is the prospects or the wisdom of multilateralizing the problem.

Maybe we didn't all agree, but what I had said earlier is we're not the only victim, and they're not the only perpetrator. One of the things that this administration has done in other contexts, which I think has been very effective, is to develop multilateral coalitions. In fact, one of the things, speaking from the standpoint of the business community, that both impressed me and surprised me was the extent to which both the European and the American business community mobilized on the indigenous innovation issue to get governments collectively on both sides of the Atlantic to apply pressure to the Chinese government, at the same time, in the same way, on the same issues with the same asks and getting the companies to do the same thing.

I think we're going to try and do the same thing now with the Indians. We'll see if that works.

But is this an area where that is possible? Is it an area where it is wise? Is it an area that may be not possible right now because of, as Dr. Mulvenon put it, the recent unpleasantness?

Vice Chairman Shea, go first.

VICE CHAIRMAN SHEA: I just wanted to ask you a question, ChairmanChairman Reinsch. I tend to agree, multilateral--it's better to go with a group than on your own--but has it really made a significant impact on indigenous innovation? At the central level, you hearthere's a spotty record at the provincial level.

I'm just curious as to--

CHAIRMAN REINSCH: I have a view, but I'll defer to the panelists.

DR. MULVENON: Well, my discussions with people that, for instance, the fights we've had about the Government Procurement Regulations and things like that, was very striking.

Was it three years ago December, two-and-a-half years ago December, when 30 plus international trade associations had a public letter to the Ministers of Finance and Commerce in China basically saying, we're finding it difficult to make money in this country, and we don't believe that the Chinese economic structure is maturing in the way we thought it would have after 30 years, that we could all have win-win scenarios and make money together, and it's still very predatory, and the regulatory system is still very predatory, and the cozy relationships between ministries and their former commercial enterprises is still too cozy.

But we have had some successes, I think, in particular, on government procurement and other things, and I think it's emboldened those, that coalition of trade associations, to look at other issues. The only problem we have, and again even before the recent "unpleasantness," as we say in the South, is the fact that some of the host governments of some our multilateral allies are themselves engaged in rampant economic espionage, so there is a bit of a conflict of interests on some of those issues. I'm thinking of the French, in particular.

CHAIRMAN REINSCH: There is so much room for hypocrisy.

DR. MULVENON: Yes, there is. "Your winnings, Monsieur." Exactly right.

[Laughter.]

CHAIRMAN REINSCH: Let's come back to my question, if we can. I mean is this something we should do, and if so, how do we do it? Mr. Quinn.

MR. QUINN: Well, I will just say that, in general, the cooperation between companies is very good. So when you look at trade issues, when you look at regulatory issues here in the United States, elsewhere around the world, it's very easy for us through associations to get together and work to overcome hurdles that a particular country puts in front of us together. Once we're past that hurdle and it's time to compete again, we're right back at going at each other, like cats and dogs.

But in my experience, particularly focused on China, very easy for us to get the EU Chamber together with the U.S. Chamber, with the American Chamber, and with the other chambers, and then even break that out into private discussions and work together to overcome those initial hurdles that are placed in our way, and then we can compete once again.

VICE CHAIRMAN SHEA: Why has this not happened if it's so

relatively easy? Or has it happened, and I'm just not aware of it?

DR. MULVENON: Well, I think, I mean the U.S. Chamber is very focused on this issue. I've attended a dozen meetings on this subject.

VICE CHAIRMAN SHEA: Sure.

DR. MULVENON: But I think that there was a time lag. I really think that we've been fighting Chinese IT standards, bullying, and we've been fighting government procurement and indigenous innovation for six, seven, eight years. The coalescence on the cybersecurity issue has been more recent.

But it's certainly no less, particularly now that their feeling is that the U.S. government is squarely behind it. I mean keep in mind that the White House Cyber Czar job was set up to be dual-hatted to the economic people and the national security people on purpose by Larry Summers because he knew cybersecurity was going to be expensive, and he didn't want to upset the economic recovery.

So there was a time very recently in this town when the economic and trade departments were wary of fording into the cybersecurity river because they thought that it was potentially going to be harmful to economic recovery and other things.

As I said to the Chinese in the last iteration of our Dialogue, I said you've really done something remarkable, and they all sat up in their chairs like, "well, what have we done?" "Is it our manned space program? Is it the Olympics?" I said, "no." I said, "as a political scientist, you've done something I thought was heretofore impossible. Your intrusion set has been so brazen in its scope and scale, you've actually compelled a unified whole-of-government response from the American government." I mean political scientists everywhere are astonished.

[Laughter.]

DR. MULVENON: But I think that signal and seeing it elevated at the S&ED and other things has also told the Chamber and other bodies that, in fact, the Chinese are not going to be able to divide and conquer on the issue between the government and our issues on currency and other things being a higher priority, and I think that's why we're finally having some traction on it.

To me, we're still in the 'what do we do about it?' I mean that's why we're having this roundtable. The business community is spending a lot of time saying to themselves, "okay, even if we meet collectively, what collectively do we want to do about it?" And people are trying to put those ideas on the table right now.

CHAIRMAN REINSCH: Well, that is the private sector. What about multiple governments? Are we in a position these days to try to create a global coalition on cyber integrity? Who wants to answer that? You're the designated victim.

MR. KAMPHAUSEN: Yeah. At one level, we're a victim of our persuasiveness. We have convinced the Chinese and other potential adversaries in this dimension that we believe so strongly in this problem because our country's national security is directly hinged to our economic security, the vibrancy, the recovery of our economy, and so forth. And so the two are inextricably linked.

And the Chinese say in response we completely agree. We're using all the tools available to us to bring about enhanced national security through a more vibrant economy. Why aren't you?

And we've, in their mind, we have self-limited. Now we have very good reasons for why we've done this. And I'm not suggesting or even beginning to argue, that we ought to fundamentally change how we do business. But I'm answering the question of how likely is it that we'll be able to multilateralize on this response?

I don't know if we'll find another partner who makes the same distinctions that Dr. Mulvenon talks about earlier between economic-- government sanctioned economic espionage and government sanctioned national security espionage.

COMMISSIONER WESSEL: Let me ask a more direct question, which goes back to the recent unpleasantness, but I'll broaden it to the Snowden affair, et cetera, you know, cyber was on the front page of every paper, and we were, the Chinese had unified the American government. Now, the American government and many others are on their heels a bit because of the Snowden affair.

What impact has that had on the ability to address the commercial side of this? You know, it's not on the front page anymore, and everyone is saying, well, your hands are a little dirty. We can't trust you. You say that it's only on the intelligence side but not on the commercial side. Is there any trust out there? Has that affair created such a gap that the ability to multilateralize this has been set back?

DR. MULVENON: Well, there is nothing so annoying as a situation in which either inadvertently or on purpose you hand the Chinese something that allows them to be really gratingly self-righteous, and they're going to sort of wallow in this for awhile, and I don't really think we're going to make a lot of progress for awhile on this issue.

It's really, I would say it's probably going to delay progress six to 12 months, and if "he-who-must-not-be-named" continues to sort of trickle out this material, it could go on for a long, long time. That's not to say that other people are not looking at the Chinese high dudgeon reaction and going "please," you know, "really."

But there is a real disconnect on the Chinese side about this issue and an inability to talk about it in public that is reasonable. I think it's the nature of their political system that doesn't allow them to have this kind of honest conversation, but simply going to the podium and saying, you know, we can neither confirm nor deny the allegations about Unit 61398, but we as a rule do not discuss intelligence operations from this podium. Boom, that easy; right?

Instead the Chinese reaction through the official Ministry of National Defense spokesman was there is no Unit 61398, which is

Kafkaesque almost in its sort of obfuscation, particularly given the hundreds of pieces of open source evidence that we have provided either through Mandiant or other places that, in fact, that's exactly who those guys are and their resumes and their skill sets and everything else, and so as long as that's the discussion where we can't, where they won't even acknowledge physical reality, much less own up to what we don't expect them to own up to, we're going to have a very hard road on this.

You can see it in the comments from the Cyber Working Group and from the comments at the S&ED and the comments at the Foreign Ministry--they really feel like they have us over a barrel at this point on this issue. There's going to have to be a dramatic change, probably another thing on the order of the Mandiant Report exposing new revelations about their behavior that finally restores some sort of equilibrium.

CHAIRMAN REINSCH: Well, maybe the three of you could comment. Is it your collective view that right now for any of the reasons you just said, a dialogue is really a waste of time? We shouldn't be spending our time on this?

DR. MULVENON: No, no, no.

CHAIRMAN REINSCH: We should be spending our time on the other recommendations of the Commission?

DR. MULVENON: Well, again, cyber is a multifaceted issue, and we have made progress on other critical aspects of it. They may not be directly related to the issue of IP theft, but as a deliverable for the Sunnylands Summit, the Chinese made a dramatic reversal on their view about how the laws of armed conflict didn't apply to the cyber dimension, which was a showstopper for DoD about it being involved in any confidence building measures or anything like that.

So even though that's not directly related to the economic issue, given what I said earlier about how the Chinese don't make the same cute distinction, it is absolutely on point that we are making progress on some elements of the cyber dimension with them.

At the same time, there are other things that you may not think are relevant to this issue, but, in fact, are, in particular, the fights we're having with them about the nature and future of global Internet governance. That's actually going to have a very dramatic effect on our ability to develop international coalitions on commercial espionage because if we move global Internet governance from organizations like ICANN and other sort of informal coalitions that include nongovernmental economic organizations, and it gets moved to a place like the U.N. International Telecommunication Union, which is a state-centered body where most of the countries agree with China's view about cyber sovereignty and everything else, we will have a lot more difficulty frankly making progress on even some of these economic and trade relationships because the nature of the multilateral governance system will have changed in ways that I think is deleterious to our interests.

CHAIRMAN REINSCH: That's actually something my other organization worked on a lot. In fact, I think we may have sent somebody to it.

DR. MULVENON: To WCIT.

CHAIRMAN REINSCH: Yes, to WCIT. The problem, of course, is that the Chinese are not the only ones. In fact, they are probably in some respects not the worst in terms of advocating a global Internet regime that involves a much higher level of government control and intrusion than the United States has supported.

It is, also, though, an area where the business community and the U.S. government are clearly of one mind and working together.

Roy.

MR. KAMPHAUSEN: Mr. Chairman, your question was do you all, how would you react to the notion that right now a dialogue would be a waste of time?

And at one level, I completely agree with Dr. Mulvenon, that it's very difficult to say something is fundamentally and completely a waste of time when there are so many dimensions to it. So it makes sense to do it for the reasons he said. But I think the premise of the question, intentionally or not, suggests that we can negotiate our way to a solution of this problem.

In other words, the conditions need to be right for us to get to a solution, and then the problem will be largely mitigated or disappear entirely. And I think it's fair to say the Commission would say they don't see that as a likely outcome, and thus the very important emphasis on the unilateral steps the United States has to take in its own interests almost independent of what the status of a dialogue is.

There are enormous risks that are associated with that, and the commissioners are well aware of that, but they are not taken with the notion that we can, this is a soluable problem the solution to which will be arrived through negotiation.

CHAIRMAN REINSCH: Mr. Quinn, you want to add anything? Or are you in the same place?

MR. QUINN: I would say, again, from our point of view, this is a pragmatic problem, something we deal with on a daily basis. I think it's one of a number of business issues that we have to take into account, and it's a problem that we need to manage.

We certainly would say that and recommend that the government continue to have a dialogue with all governments, including the Chinese, multilateral. If I was the government employee that was somehow put in charge of this, I'd be reaching out everywhere I could to try to put it together and find the right vehicle that's going to get us the most traction. It just needs to continue. We're going to have revelations of things happening and coming and going, but the dialogue needs to continue.

I think from our point of view, again, for us it's a practical issue that we need to deal with, and so we would want to see the government at the highest levels continuing that dialogue, but also at the same time, trying to work with the business community to come up with strategies that we can begin to implement more quickly to protect ourselves, share information, and to handle these day-in and day-out ramifications of what's going on.

CHAIRMAN REINSCH: Anything to add? Okay. Actually, we've done all this with, in fact, with only my first question, and Craig has kindly prepared 27 other ones, but let me ask one last one, if I may, because we do have a couple minutes if people will forebear just to see what you have to say.

This relates to one of the things that--Dr. Mulvenon alluded to it when he talked about internal unity-- inside the United States government. Let's pursue that just a little bit more, and maybe some people will have something else to say about it that will also be wise.

What are the key roadblocks to developing effective U.S. cyber policy to prevent intrusions, and how can those roadblocks be overcome? So think about it as an internal U.S. government problem. What do we need to do or is it so severe that we've overcome all roadblocks now?

DR. MULVENON: Well, I mean let's congratulate ourselves a little bit. One of the major roadblocks when I started at looking at this 15, 20 years ago was the lack of any dialogue between law enforcement and intelligence; right. And then we stood up the National, you know, NCIJTF, and that nexus is working much better than it ever has in my experience because it's no longer a "my data went down a law enforcement hole" versus "my data went down an intel hole" and the two of them aren't talking to one another.

So that was a significant issue. The second significant hurdle was this cleavage between the national security people and the econ and trade people. I think because of the brazenness of the intrusion set, that that divide has been broken down although clearly they're pursuing different remedies.

There is a divide between those who want to pursue largely diplomatic solutions, who believe that, for instance, the Chinese have agreed to this cyber working group, therefore we don't necessarily need to hit them low anymore. My only point was the only reason they went to the open track is because we were hitting them high and hitting them low, and so we have to guard against the complacency that might come from abandoning some of the other activities that I think were causing a certain amount of pain internally, and so--

CHAIRMAN REINSCH: Mr. Kamphausen, what did the Commission have to say about this?

MR. KAMPHAUSEN: Well, I think in our interaction with folks on the Hill, two significant roadbocks are civil liberties and privacy lobbyists who take their positions to an extreme. Any effort to institute prudent controls is regarded as an affront to civil liberties or any effort to maintain information has privacy implications, and those are certainly valid and important issues, but they can be taken to an extreme. I think those are two of the key challenges that folks are facing on various committee staffs as they try to formulate legislation.

So that's one piece. The second is the structural one, and we talked about it earlier. The Commission made a recommendation as to who the best leader would be and what the composite organizations ought to be drawn from. I think we have seen enough success with those sorts of interagency working groups over time and in different venues that that's less an obstacle conceptionally than it is an obstacle practically, just getting the gears turning to put that into effect, where do you house it, how do you staff it, how do you draw from the other interagency players, all those sorts of things.

But we've demonstrated we know how to do it. We just have to set those wheels in motion. There is maybe a more fundamental disconnect, and that is really the basic one is are we going to get our way through the problem with more or less government intervention or are we going to get our way through the problem with more or less reliance on the market to solve the problems for itself?

And, you know, it seems to us that it's a negotiated path that consists of pieces from each part, but that will likely bog down the progress that folks are making as they try to produce legislation. I think that kind of central theoretical question.

CHAIRMAN REINSCH: Okay. Anybody want to add anything? Mr. Quinn and then--

MR. QUINN: Just a couple of things I guess. Again, I think from our point of view what we'd like to have is a point of contact within the government that allows us to share information and also gather information. If you look at Rockwell Automation, we're a big company, but we've got a little, close to 5,000 small and medium-sized companies that provide us components that go into our products.

We have 300,000 products in our catalogue, and so these companies are constantly pushing this material to us. We have the wherewithal to go out and hire consultants and do deep dives into our systems, protect ourselves as best as possible. We have contacts with the government. Primarily those have been individually developed over time that allow us to discuss things from time to time in more detail than we might otherwise do.

But these small and medium-size companies that funnel into us, that are critical to us being successful, they don't have that access. These companies come from all over the United States. Some of them are producing internationally, some in China, some elsewhere, but I really think that there is a need for an office, and I'm not against the Commerce Department. I think it's a very accessible agency, and they're already set up to meet with businesses and talk to them.

The FCS is a great organization, in a way. Train up the officers a little bit differently, but they need to be linked into their brothers in the government that have access to this information. You know it doesn't have to be detailed information, but it has to be enough that they can sensitize these small and medium-size manufacturers to the threat and make recommendations to them if they're looking at entering certain markets, how to best protect themselves, what to look for, what are the red flags.

I think another way that the government can help is, look, you're great at research and development. You know, you look at we're doing a lot of work with DARPA, ARPA-E, and others today in a myriad of areas. We could be working in the same area--the government putting seed money understanding what the threat is. They're the best access. They know what the bad guys have out there. They can identify it, work with companies to then develop technologies to offset that, and make those commercially available.

You know, private companies are doing it. I know that. They're involved in it. But could the government help out with that, I think they could as well.

CHAIRMAN REINSCH: Excellent. Time is up. Vice Chairman Shea, Commissioner Wessel, do you have anything to say at the end?

VICE CHAIRMAN SHEA: No. Fine. Thank you.

COMMISSIONER WESSEL: No, other than thank you for your time.

VICE CHAIRMAN SHEA: Yes. Thank you.

CHAIRMAN REINSCH: And I was going to say thank you very much. For me, this has been an exceptionally rich and thoughtful discussion. The Commission is charged--our Commission--as well as yours is charged with making recommendations to the Congress, and our Annual Report will be out in November, and I'm sure this is going to be a significant part of it.

And to the extent that is so, we have you to thank, and so we're very grateful for not only your time, but we're grateful for your wise thoughts and your interest in the issue, and there may possibly be follow up in which case we hope that you'll indulge us in that, too.

So with that, thank you very much, and we're adjourned.

[Whereupon, at 11:05 a.m., the roundtable was adjourned.]